TEACH YOURSELF TO PLAY

PIANO
SONGS

To access audio visit:
www.halleonard.com/mylibrary
Enter Code
7484-6983-2593-4443

ISBN 978-1-4950-3586-9

HAL•LEONARD®
CORPORATION
7777 W. BLUEMOUND RD. P.O. BOX 13819 MILWAUKEE, WI 53213

Visit Hal Leonard Online at
www.halleonard.com

TEACH YOURSELF LESSON

BENNIE AND THE JETS

Take a look at the introduction to this abridged version of an Elton John classic. The eighth note chords followed by eighth rests create the rhythmic chord stabs that make this tune so recognizable. In the right hand, two chords, Gmaj7 and Fmaj7 are separated by a distinctive rhythmic motive. The chords are just one note apart from each other. The left hand plays bass notes (same note names as the chords) joined with a bit of chromatic movement for interest and color.

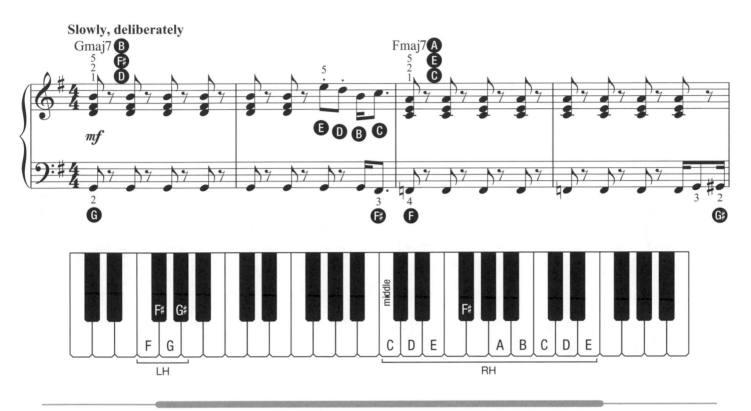

Heading into the verse, you'll see that your right hand stays in pretty much one place. What's tricky though, is moving through the **accidentals** (sharps, flats and naturals outside the key signature). Just like in the left-hand part of the introduction, this adds color to both melody and harmony. Before playing each part separately, take a minute to find the chromatic notes on the keyboard. For right hand, find A♯ and F♮, and for left hand, find E to E♭ to D, and G to G♯.

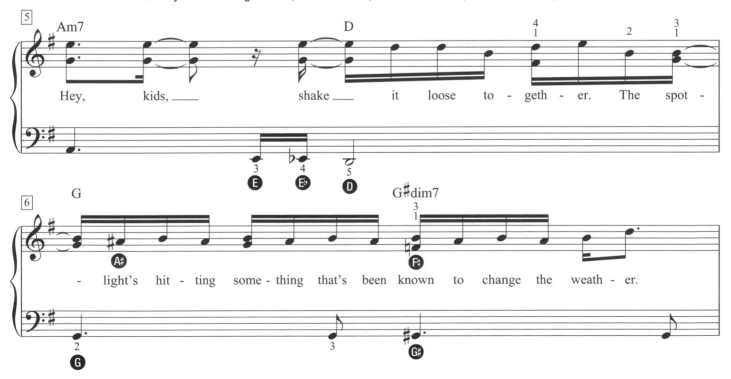

At the chorus, "Bennie and the Jets" (m. 13) the left hand changes to mostly quarter notes, really emphasizing a steady pulse, and making it easy to see where the right-hand rhythms line up.

Jump ahead to the instrumental interlude at measure 19. Sir Elton likes to alternate chords over repeating bass notes. We've marked the chords for you below. Practice each hand separately if you need to, and use the online audio to really feel the rhythmic groove here.

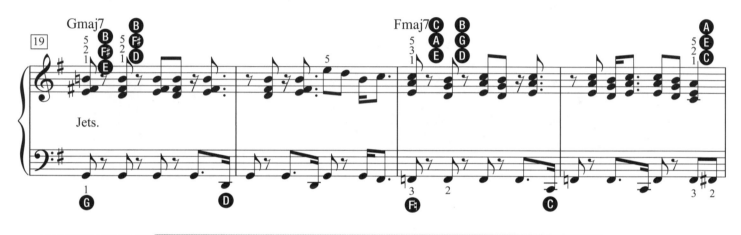

Continue on through the ending, putting together chords, rhythms and chromatic notes. You're ready to play the whole arrangement!

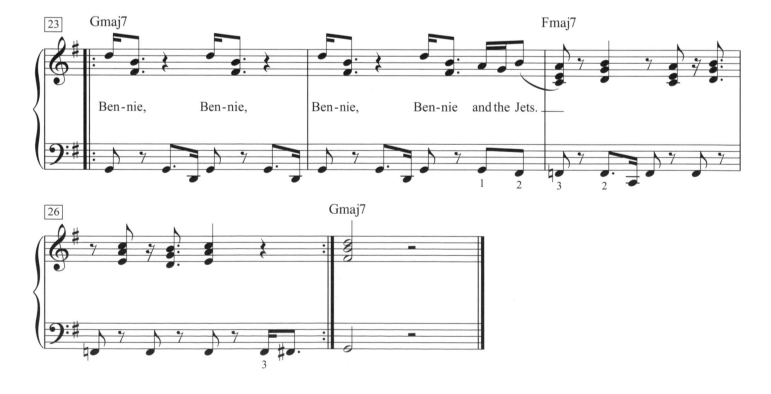

BENNIE AND THE JETS

Words and Music by ELTON JOHN
and BERNIE TAUPIN

Slowly, deliberately

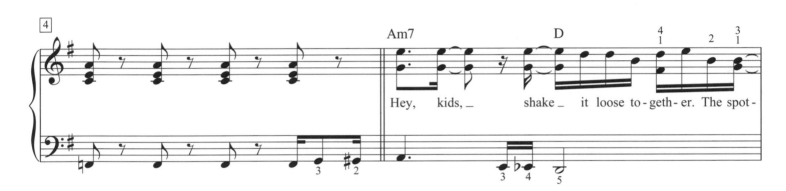

Hey, kids, _ shake _ it loose to-geth-er. The spot-

-light's hit-ting some-thing that's been known to change the weath-er.

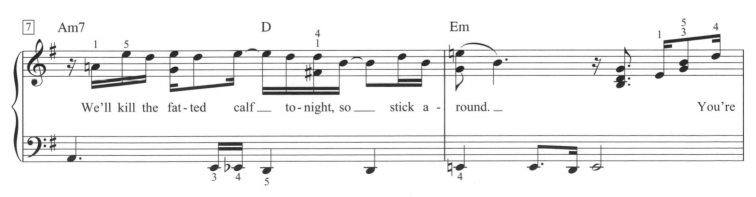

We'll kill the fat-ted calf _ to-night, so _ stick a-round. _ You're

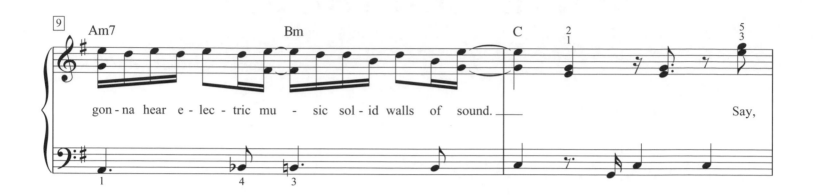

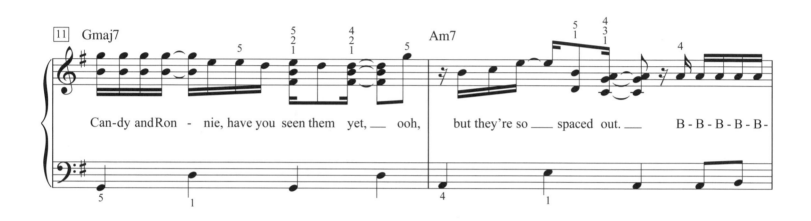

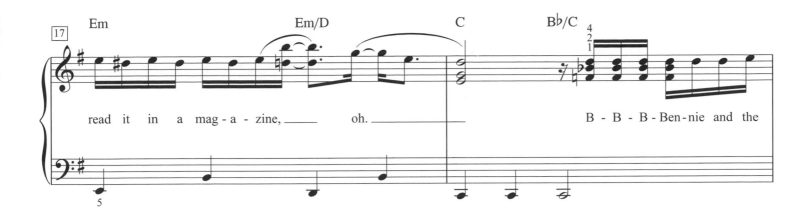

read it in a mag - a - zine, _____ oh. _____ B - B - B - Ben - nie and the

Jets.

Ben - nie, Ben - nie, Ben - nie, Ben - nie and the Jets. _____

CENTERFOLD

This J. Geils Band hit uses the chord progression C-B♭-F almost exclusively throughout the entire song. Finding and identifying this pattern will make learning this song super quick.

The introduction illustrates this clearly. The left hand plays open fifths. The right hand's playful melody is easy if you follow the fingering we've highlighted here. A quick finger substitution from thumb on middle C to third finger on middle C gets you where you need to go.

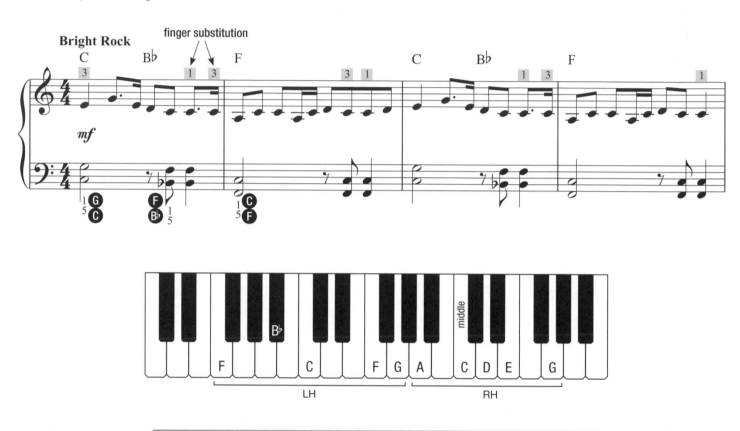

As you head into the verse, notice that the left hand continues to play open fifths, but there's a bit of a change in the pattern. After C-B♭, the next measure has a quick switch: F-B♭-F, instead of staying only with F for the entire measure. Be sure to emphasize the right hand joining in on the B♭-F chord, for extra rhythmic drive.

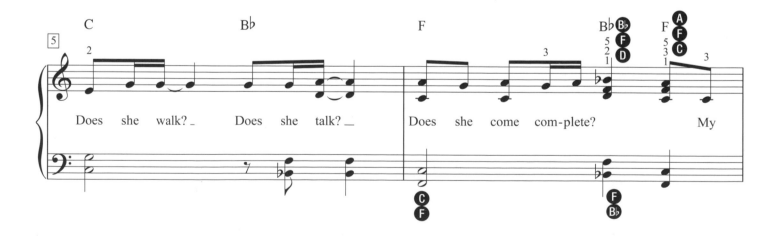

There's a change at measure 13. The progression is: Am-Dm-F-G. This repeats before returning to our familiar C-B♭-F. Take a moment to practice the left-hand part before playing it with the melody.

Enjoy the rhythmic interplay in right and left hands in measures 17-20, repeated in measures 21-24. Right hand is syncopated, and left hand supplies the answering rhythmic emphasis.

Close out this classic with a repeated ending, and finish strong. Don't forget to sing along!

CENTERFOLD

Written by
SETH JUSTMAN

GOODBYE YELLOW BRICK ROAD

This Elton John ballad is one of his biggest hits. To get this under your fingers, let's divide our abridged arrangement into three parts, beginning with part one, the first 16 measures.

To learn the left-hand part quickly, note the chord labels above the treble staff. The notes in the left hand almost always match the chord name. As you learn the left-hand part, consider playing along with the right-hand online audio.

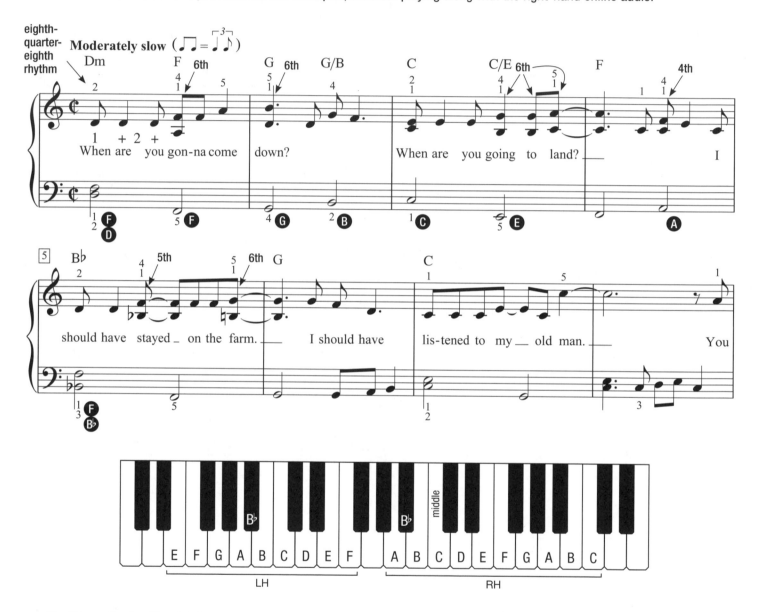

You'll hear the familiar eighth note-quarter note-eighth note syncopation in the right-hand melody. Notice some 4ths, 5ths and 6ths in the right hand to fill out the harmony. We've marked both of these things in the example above. When the left hand feels secure, add the right hand.

Measures 9-16 has the same left-hand part, so jump into the right-hand part, looking for similarities to the first eight measures.

You'll see the addition of the accidentals A♭, B♭, and E♭ in the next section. The chord labels above the treble staff will again be a help in learning the left hand. The right hand uses the interval of a blocked 6th quite a bit. Keep your hand shape the same, and "slide" from note to note. You'll move to a higher octave on the keyboard, as indicated on the keyboard diagram below.

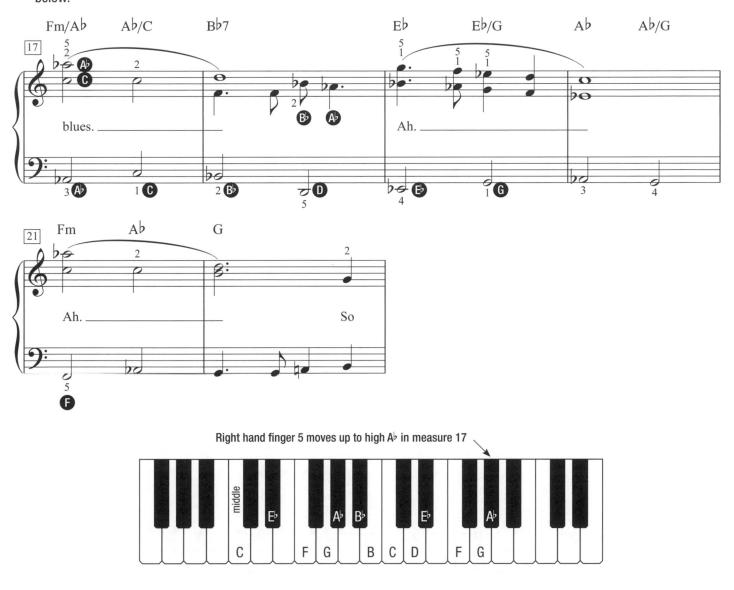

Right hand finger 5 moves up to high A♭ in measure 17

Continuing with the lyrics, "Good-bye yellow brick road…" you'll see quite a bit of familiar material. Bass notes continue to match the chord labels, and the right hand uses the distinctive eighth-quarter-eighth rhythm, and lots of 6ths.

Use the online audio as your personal tutor while you continue to put the rest of this song together. Review rhythms, and check the accuracy of the accidentals. You can loop small sections for repeated practice, and slow down the tempo as needed.

GOODBYE YELLOW BRICK ROAD

Words and Music by ELTON JOHN
and BERNIE TAUPIN

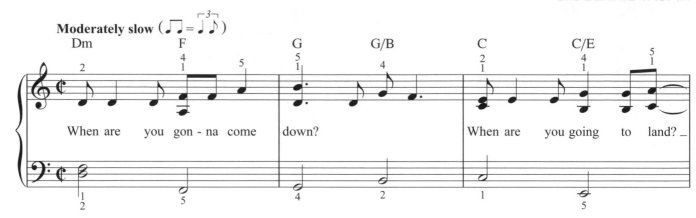

When are you gon - na come down? When are you going to land?

I should have stayed on the farm. I should have

lis - tened to my old man. You know you can't hold me for - ev -

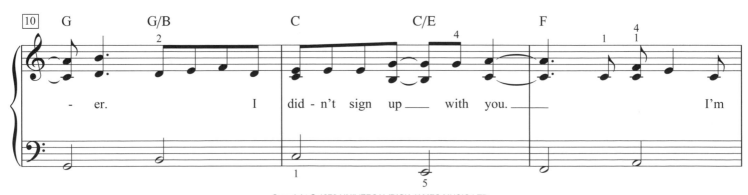

- er. I did - n't sign up with you. I'm

TEACH YOURSELF LESSON

HEY JUDE

This all-time favorite Beatles classic relies on the left hand to keep things moving. For the first eight measures the left hand plays 5ths on the keyboard. Practice moving your left hand as we've illustrated below.

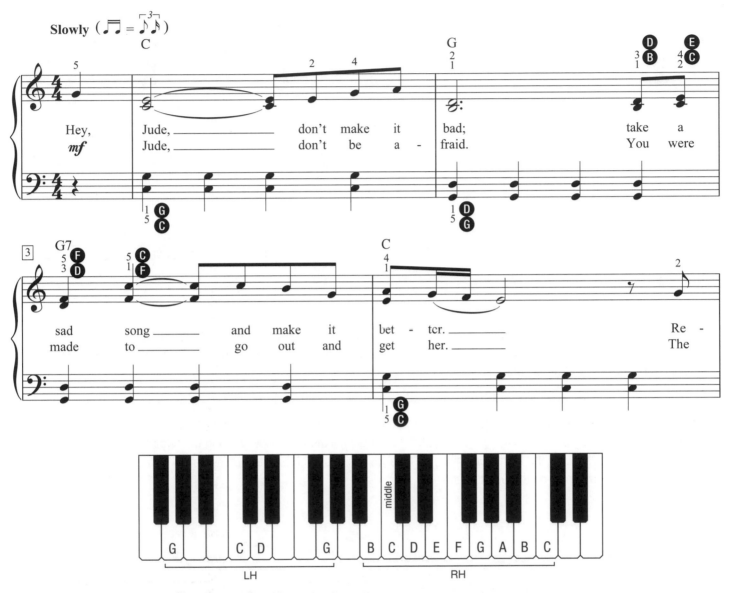

Next, take a closer look at the right-hand melody in the example above. First, isolate the thirds on the lyrics "take a sad song." Notice how the thirds fall under the hand so as the notes step up, you play with consecutive fingers. When you have used up all your fingers, jump to the fifth by transferring finger 1 to the F that finger 5 just played. Study the fingering given and play in slow motion at first.

Continuing on with the second ending we begin a new section. The left-hand intervals get much more interesting, starting with the 7th in measure 10, and then building from 5th-6th-7th back to 6ths in measures 11-13.

Use the online audio to check your right hand notes, or if you need a rhythm review. Singing along with the lyrics will also help with the tied notes and syncopation. Once you're comfortable with measures 10-13, you can continue through measure 21, as this material repeats.

You've now learned all the notes you need to continue through the return of the lyrics, "Hey Jude…" until measure 30, at the familiar ascending chromatic notes, "better, better,…" Practice the notes slowly, using the fingering provided. Play along with the audio, slowing the tempo down as much as you need to at first. When you're comfortable with the fingering, increase the tempo, and play on through the end.

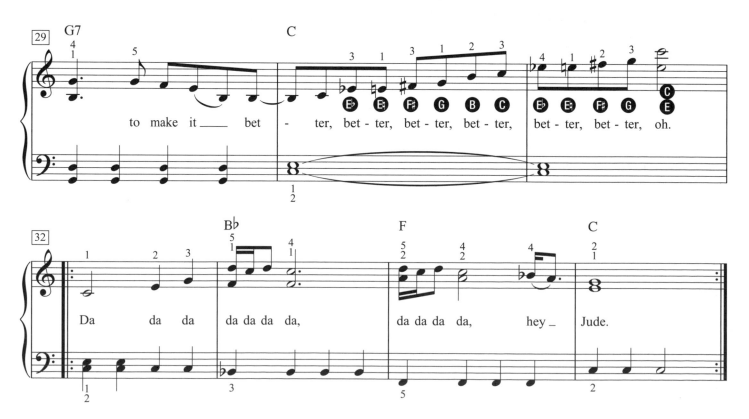

HEY JUDE

Words and Music by JOHN LENNON
and PAUL McCARTNEY

TEACH YOURSELF LESSON

PIANO MAN

Billy Joel's first hit single is a favorite with pianists everywhere. This arrangement will help you learn everything you need to know to perfect this iconic keyboard tune.

The song tells a story, so to learn the material quickly, let's look at things section by section, letting the lyrics lead us. This will make it easy to see parts that are similar. For example, measures 1-32 look like one long section, but can be divided in half, and then in half again. Learning the first eight measures provides you with much of what you need to play through to measure 32.

In the left hand, focus on the notes and also on the chord labels above the staff. "Slash" chords show the name of the chord, followed by the name of the bass note, the letter after the "slash." Work on the left hand until you can play with a steady but moving tempo, feeling each measure in one large beat. Listen to the online audio, or a Billy Joel recording to get a sense of what you're aiming for.

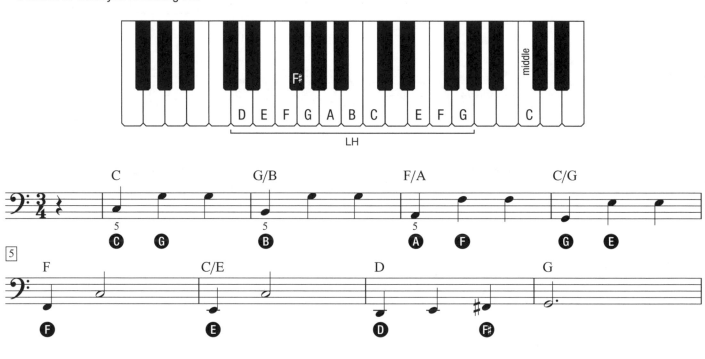

Add the right-hand melody, making note of fingering cues along the way to help you navigate changes in position, especially in measures 7-8, where the top note is held by finger 5 as lower notes change along with the bass notes.

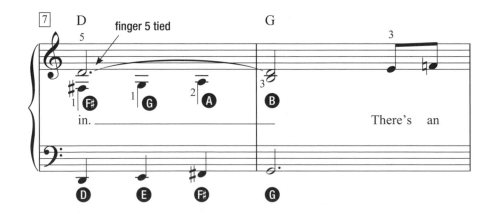

Before moving on, look through measures 9-16. You'll see that the left hand is almost exactly the same as measures 1-8, and the right hand is very similar. This is the perfect time to play from measure 1-16 with the online audio.

The next section of lyrics, beginning with the pick-up to measure 17 is just about the same as the first 16 measures, with one notable difference-your right hand is played one octave higher. Check the keyboard below.

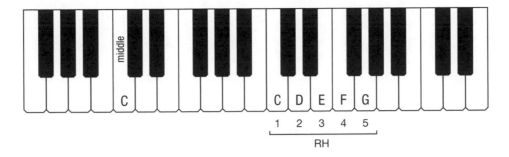

A new, contrasting section begins at measure 33. Left hand continues in the waltz pattern already established (check your chord labels for help), and the right hand moves along in 6ths.

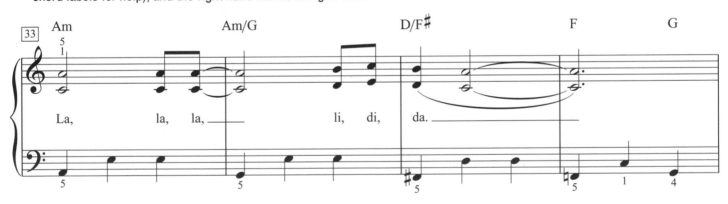

Looking ahead to measure 45, the left hand starts on a lower C than previously, but soon settles into the familiar part you learned previously. Right hand is still in the higher octave. Our arrangement concludes with the signature piano solo ending, measures 59 to the end.

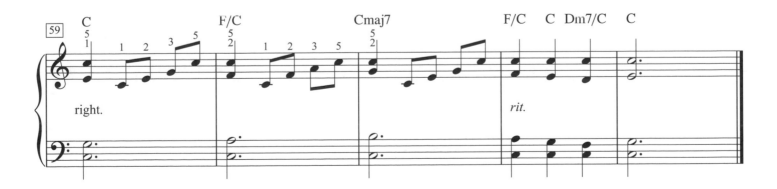

PIANO MAN

Words and Music by
BILLY JOEL

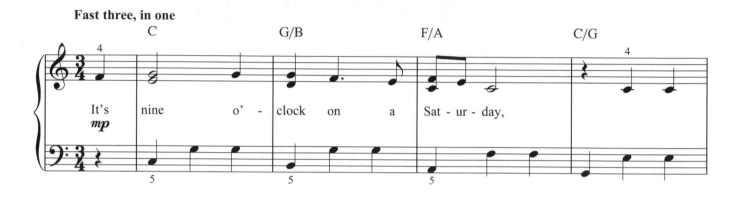

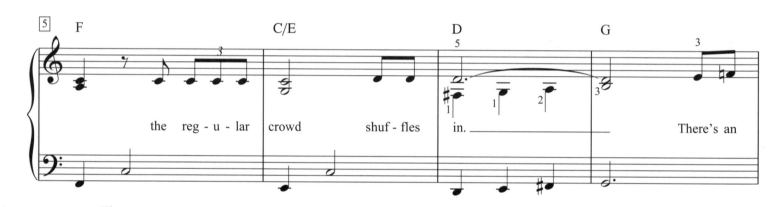

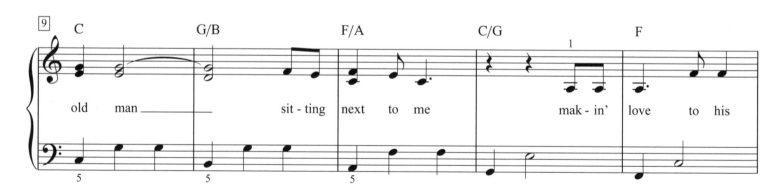

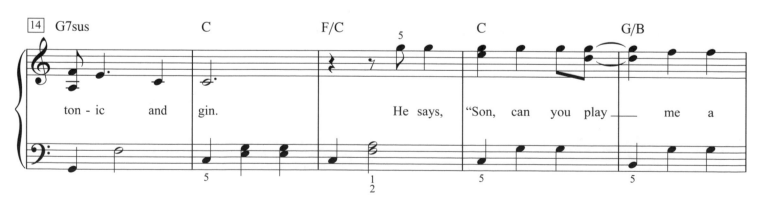

STEPPIN' OUT

One of Joe Jackson's biggest hits, "Steppin' Out" has a driving bass line that's loads of fun to play. Learn and memorize the first two measures of the left hand. You'll play this pattern 12 more times! Start on the G an octave lower than middle C.

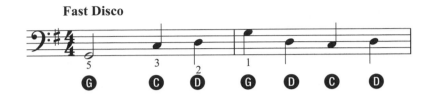

The right hand plays three-note and four-note chords. They can be quite a handful. We've added some fingering suggestions. It also helps to study where the black keys fall in each chord. Notice that F is sharp in the key signature, but it is only played sharp in the first measure of this section.

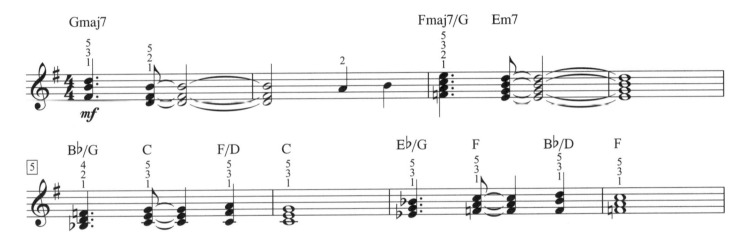

If you've memorized the left-hand part, playing hands together will be easy. If you're not quite there yet, slow the tempo down. And remember, you can use the online audio for help with this, and for playing just one hand at a time.

The left hand changes at measure nine, where the lyrics begin. Instead of the nifty two-measure pattern, you keep the rhythm driving forward with repeated notes. The pattern slips back in at measure 13, and the repeated notes start again.

Measures 9-16 is a four-measure phrase that repeats.

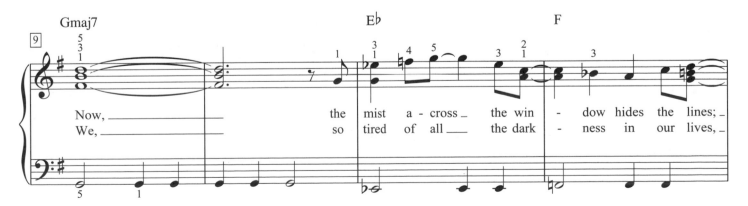

Measure 17-22 is a three-measure phrase that repeats.

This leads right into the last section. Even with the addition of lyrics, you'll recognize this material right away. It's the opening eight measures, played twice, ending with the final Gmaj9 chord.

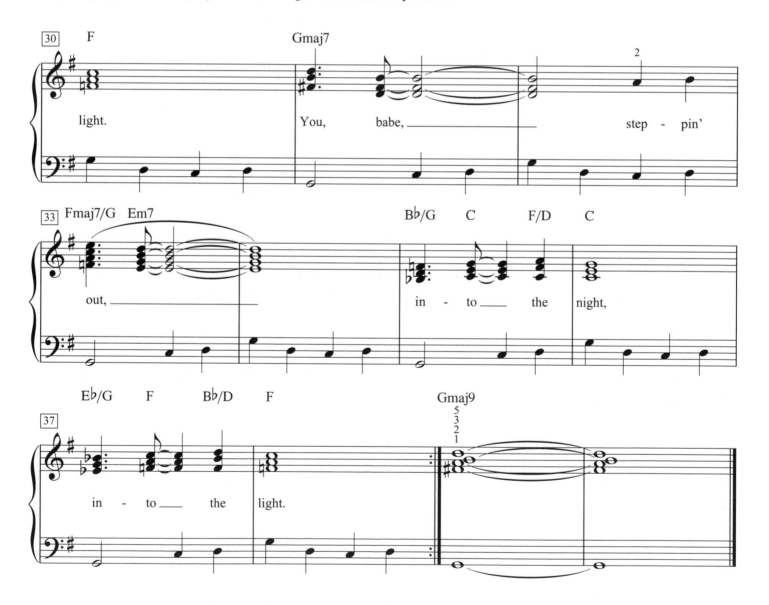

STEPPIN' OUT

Words and Music by
JOE JACKSON

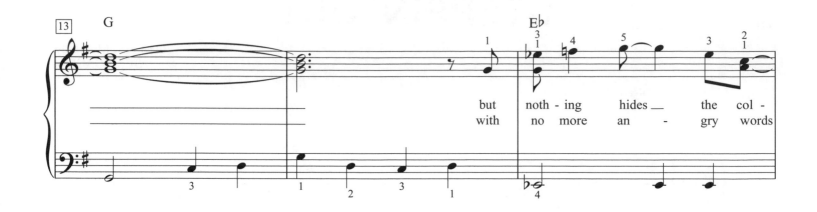

but | noth - ing | hides ___ | the | col -
with | no | more | an | - gry | words

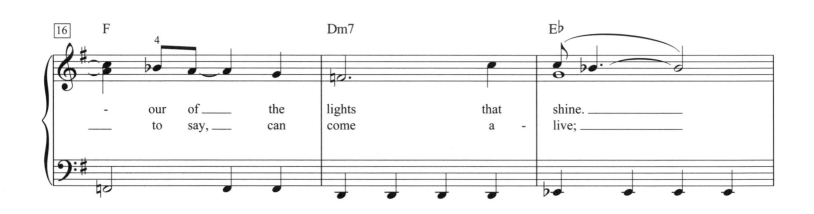

- our | of ___ | the | lights | that | shine. _____
___ | to | say, ___ | can | come | a | - live; _____

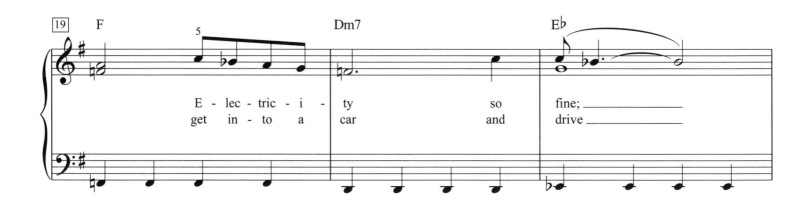

E - | lec - tric - i | - ty | so | fine; _____
get | in - to | a | car | and | drive _____

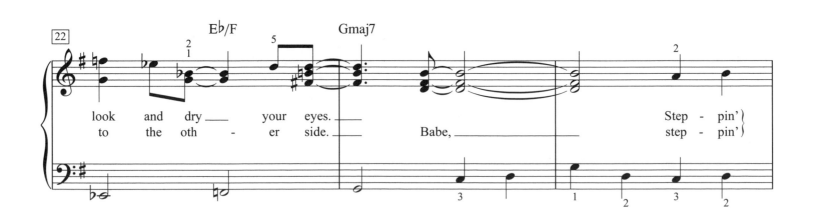

look | and | dry ___ | your | eyes. ___ | | Step - pin' }
to | the | oth | - er | side. ___ | Babe, _____ | step - pin' }

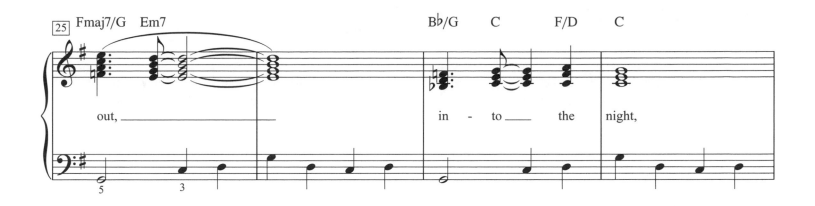

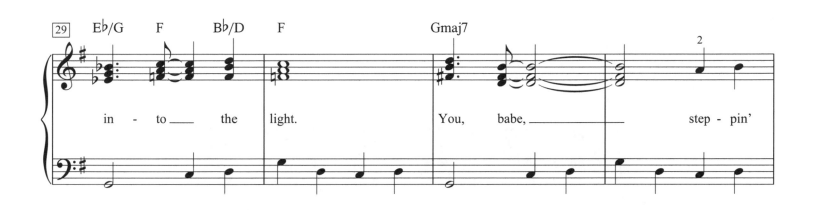

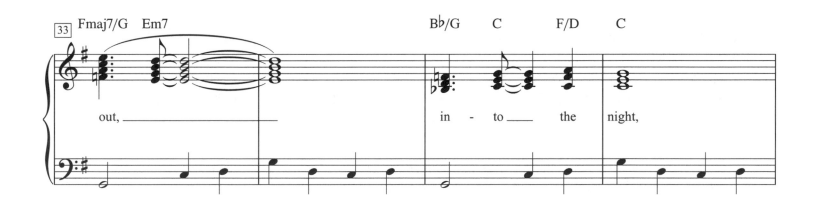

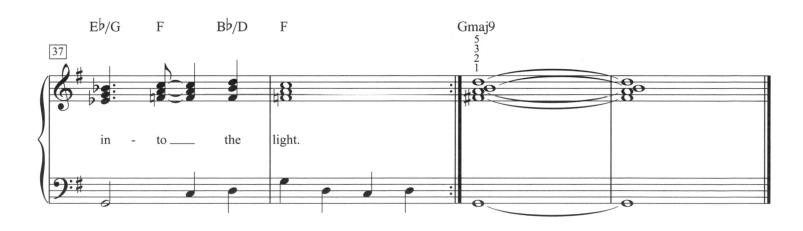

RIBBON IN THE SKY

The signature phrase of Stevie Wonder's R&B hit comes back again and again, so take some time to really study it. You might consider memorizing this phrase right off the bat. It makes a short but beautiful introduction for this arrangement. Beats 1 and 2 move in **contrary motion**, that is, opposite directions.

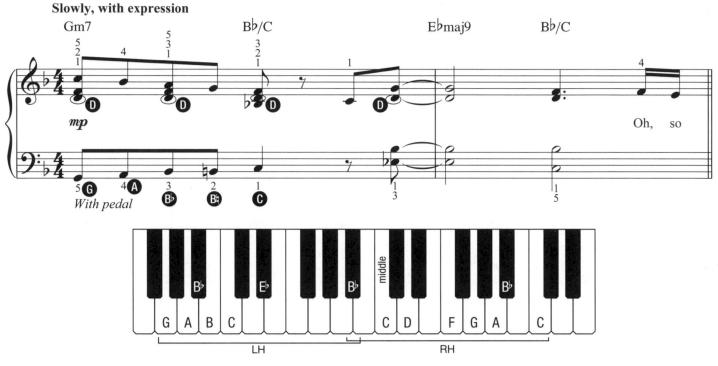

In your left hand, move up note by note, as marked in the example. Your right hand can use the note D as a reference point. D is played by thumb in the first two chords, and finger 2 in the next three chords. Remember to play B as B♭, as indicated in the key signature.

Starting in measure 3, move left-hand finger 2 to low G. You'll hang out here until the first ending, playing G, A and D in a relaxed dotted quarter-eighth pattern. Don't rush the melody of this slow ballad. Both first and second endings take you back to the "Ribbon in the Sky" phrase you learned in the introduction.

The middle section takes on a free, easily flowing feel on the lyric "doo." The left-hand 7ths continue the jazz feel, and let the 16th notes feel a bit improvisatory. Start on the G below middle C, and follow the fingering to make playing easy. Notice that this section also ends (measure 19) with the signature phrase from the introduction.

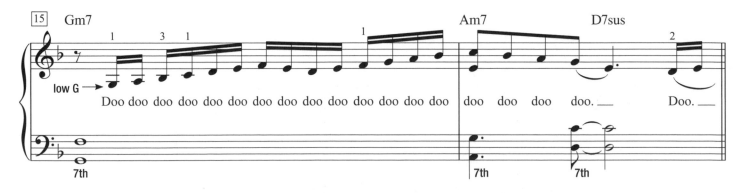

For added color and intensity, the last section is played in the key of G major, one step higher than the starting key of F major. All of the material is the same, except that all of the notes are one step higher. Instead of B♭, now you'll play all Bs as B♮, and all the Fs as F♯. Listen to the online audio to hear this transition, and play along (at a slower tempo if needed) to get a feel for the new key.

RIBBON IN THE SKY

Words and Music by
STEVIE WONDER

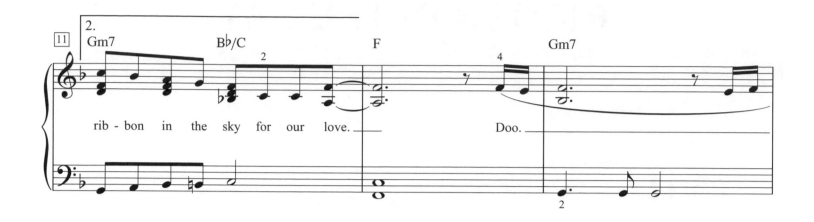

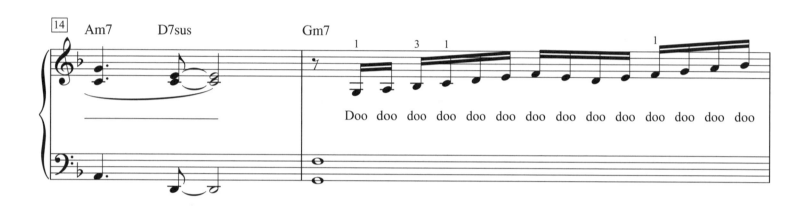

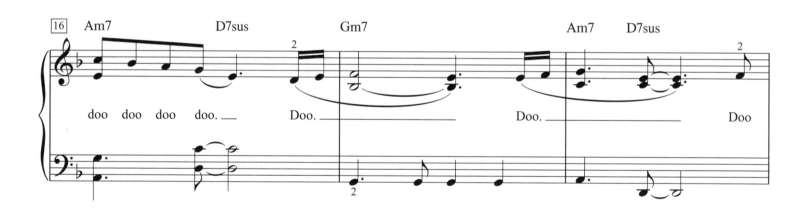

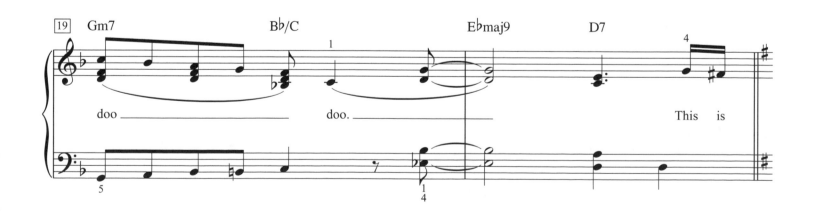

— 35 —

21
Am7
Bm7
E7sus
not a co - in - ci - dence, and far
lose, with God on our side. We'll find
23
Am7
Bm7
E7sus
Am7
more than a luck - y chance, but what is that was
strength in each tear we cry. From now on it is
26
Bm7
E7sus
1.
Am7
C/D
al - ways meant is our rib - bon's in the sky for our love.
you and I and our
28
Fmaj9
C/D
2.
Am7
C/D
We can't rib - bon in the sky,
30
Bm7♭5
E
Am7
C/D
G
rib - bon in the sky, a rib - bon in the sky for our love.

SHE'S ALWAYS A WOMAN

Billy Joel's classic love song has two parts—the first part is played three times before moving to the second part. It's important to note that the time signature denotes compound meter. The number 8 on the bottom means the eighth note gets the beat. The top number changes throughout, going from 12 to 6 to 9 before it settles into 12/8 in measure six. What this really means is that instead of many smaller beats, you'll want to have a feeling of four, three, or two larger beats per measure. Take a look at the left-hand part below, with the counting written in.

You might want to tackle each hand separately as you begin to learn the verse. The left hand starts with a solid, easy-to-play C major chord. To play Csus, use your second finger to play F instead of E. Your left hand pretty much stays in one place for the verse.

The right hand moves around a bit, but many of the phrases are similar. Note the beginning 16th notes with finger 2 on D. The second phrase starting in measure three starts exactly the same, only with finger 2 on G. The third phrase starts in measure five and you'll move finger 2 back down to D, and stay in this part of the keyboard for the rest of the verse.

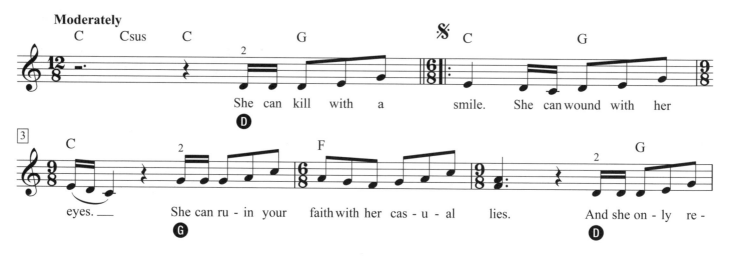

There are quite a few **sequences** in the chorus, starting at measure 10. Let's look at this closely. A sequence is a phrase or section of music that is repeated at a higher or lower pitch. Study the sequences marked in the example below.

There are more sequences in measures 14-16. Check out the left-hand fingering. Thumb crosses under twice as the notes descend.

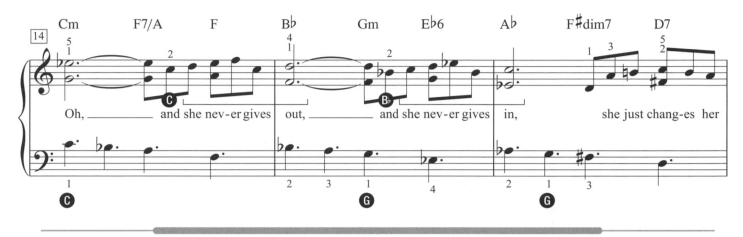

Follow the D.S. al Coda direction in measure 17 which leads back to measure 2, and then jumps ahead to the coda at the end of measure seven to end the song.

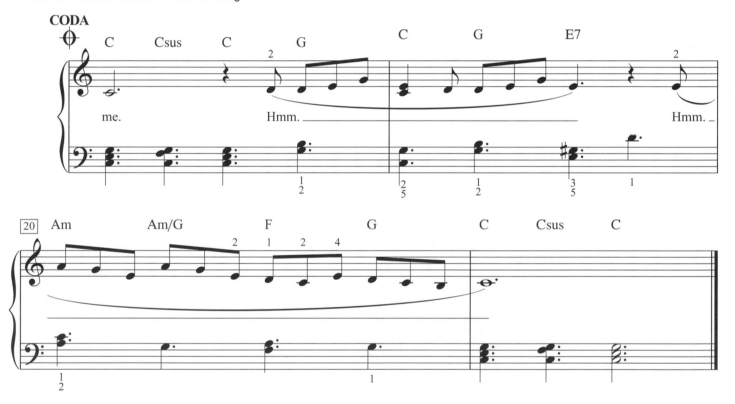

There are lots of ways to practice this song with the online audio, really hearing the groove of the compound rhythm from the beginning, and especially listening and identifying the sequences and chromatic notes in the second part.

SHE'S ALWAYS A WOMAN

Words and Music by
BILLY JOEL

9
2.
C Am D7/F♯ D7 G Em C
me. Oh, she takes care of her - self. She can wait if she
12
F Dm G7 C Cm F7/A F
wants, she's a-head of her time. Oh, and she nev-er gives
15
B♭ Gm E♭6 A♭ F♯dim7 D7
out, and she nev - er gives in, she just chang - es her
17
G G7 D.S. al Coda
mind. And she'll prom - ise you
CODA
C Csus C G
me. Hmm.
19
C G E7 Am Am/G F G C Csus C
Hmm.

YOU ARE SO BEAUTIFUL

This heartfelt song made popular by Joe Cocker begins with a lovely introduction. The tempo is slow and gentle, so don't rush the 16th notes. Identify the intervals in the left hand, keeping thumb on the D above middle C most of the time.

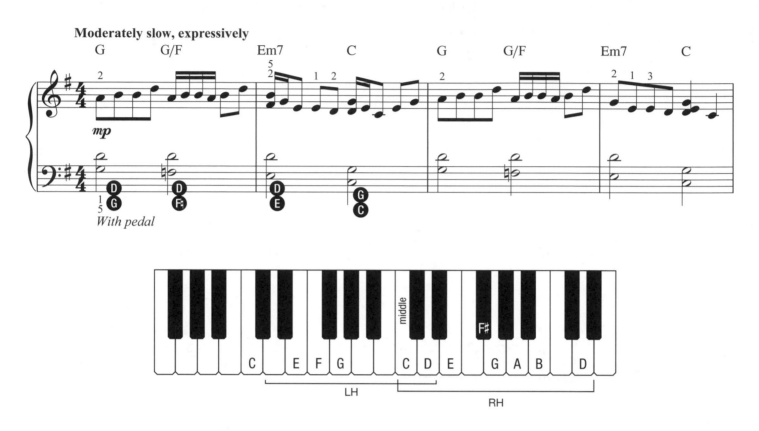

This song is built around the first phrase, "You are so beautiful…" in measures 5-8. The first three chords look like a handful, but both top and bottom notes stay the same—only the middle notes change. There's some really beautiful material between the lyrics. Play those chord changes and 16th notes expressively, and don't be afraid to stretch the rhythm a bit. Reading the ledger lines is easy if you remember that the ledger line closest to the treble clef is middle C.

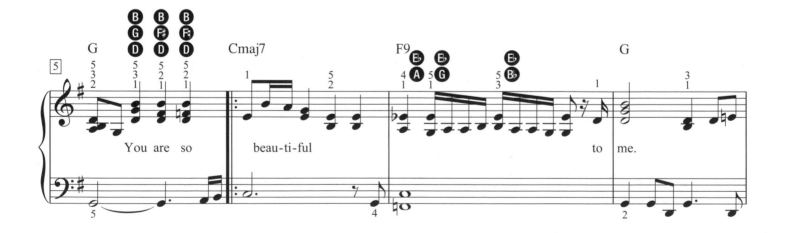

Take a look through the song and note where this phrase returns. You'll see it again beginning at measures 9, 18, and 21.

As you play through the climax of the piece, measures 14-17, you'll want to observe the fingering given to help navigate through some right-hand shifts. For example, on beat one your right hand plays near middle C. Moving your thumb to G above middle C on the next note propels you to the higher octave, leading to the B7 chord in measure 15. On beat three of this measure you shift again in order to move back to the lower octave. Study the example below, and work on the right hand separately in this section, if needed.

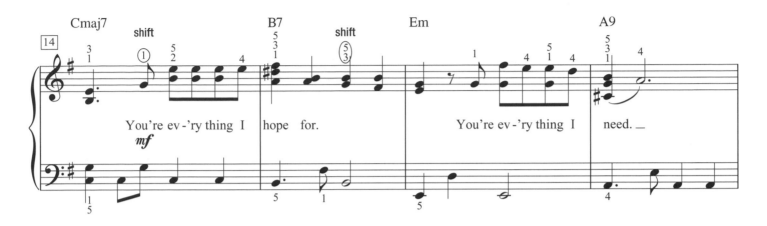

In the last section we find the lovely interlude material from the body of the song. Follow the *rit.* indication to bring this to a gradual ending, lingering on the final chord.

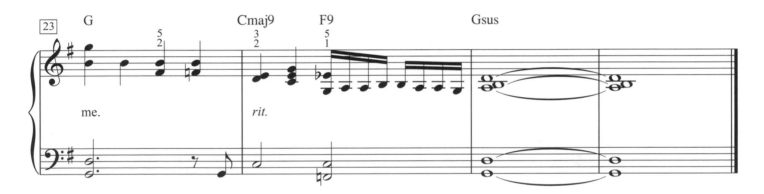

YOU ARE SO BEAUTIFUL

Words and Music by BILLY PRESTON
and BRUCE FISHER

THE WAY IT IS

Bruce Hornsby's awesome solo opens this tune with colorful harmonies and grace notes that might look a bit tricky, but fall right under your fingers. The opening eight bars are marked, "Freely," so there's no need to keep a super strict tempo here. You'll want to observe the syncopated rhythms, but use these as the framework for your own push and pull of the tempo.

The left hand is very straightforward, and in the intro, always plays the root of the chord, so let the chord labels help you out. The right hand has more to do, so let's focus on that first. Starting on the A above middle C, you'll play lots of chords and double notes, but you're never very far from G, the key in which this arrangement is written. Use the G, both upper and lower, to keep your bearings. We've highlighted it for you below.

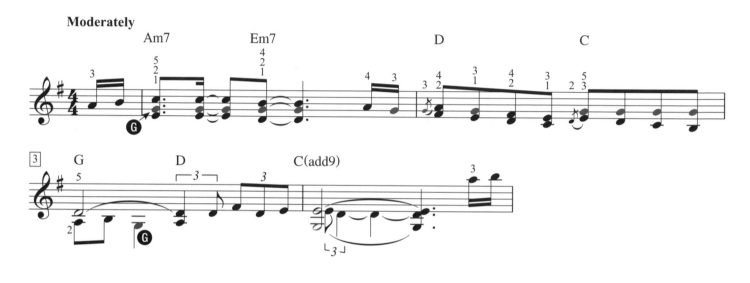

Grace notes are small notes written before the beat. Most often the grace notes are played quickly, before the note they precede, but sometimes they can be played on the beat, with the main note following, or together with the main note, and then quickly released, resulting in a slightly more dissonant, or "crunched" kind of sound. Listen to the online audio for one example of this, and then experiment on your own to find the technique and sound you prefer.

To finish the introduction, move up an octave from where you began. You'll notice much of the same material you just mastered, notated one octave higher.

At measure nine the tempo head changes to "Moderately" and these four measures lead us into the verse. Settle into a steadier tempo here, and notice again, there are many similarities to the first eight measures you've already learned.

Let's jump to measures 18-19. The right-hand part is played below and around middle C, so it's notated in the bass clef for easier reading. This short motive is played a total of four times, so take a minute to learn the notes, and practice moving from these lower notes back to the treble clef notes.

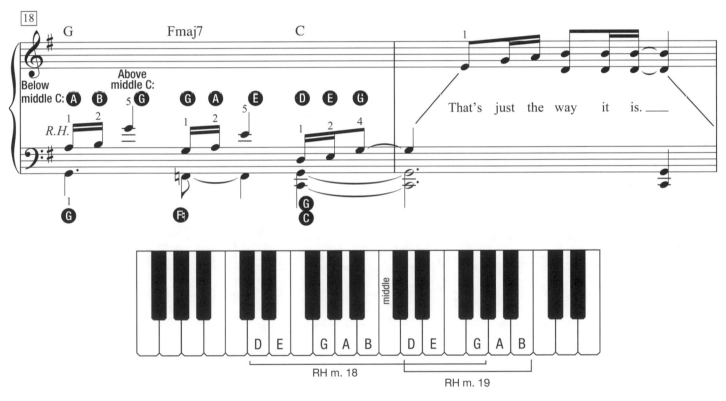

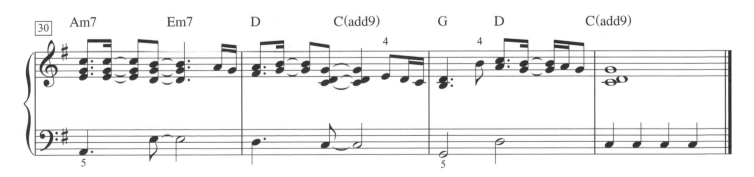

The arrangement ends with a short solo. It's the same as measures 9-12.

THE WAY IT IS

Words and Music by
BRUCE HORNSBY

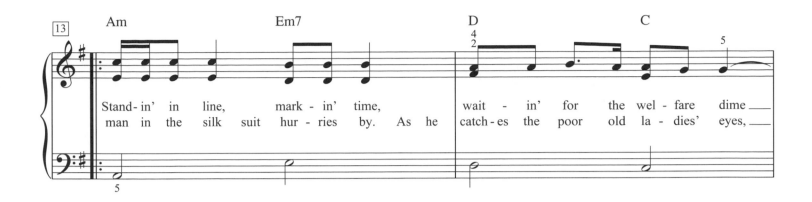

Stand-in' in line, mark-in' time, wait - in' for the wel - fare dime
man in the silk suit hur - ries by. As he catch - es the poor old la - dies' eyes,

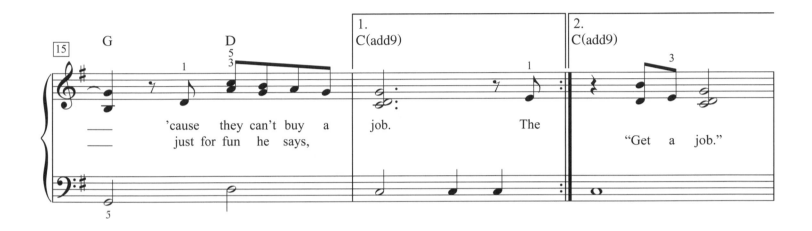

1.
C(add9)
'cause they can't buy a job. The
just for fun he says,

2.
C(add9)
"Get a job."

That's just the way it is. ___

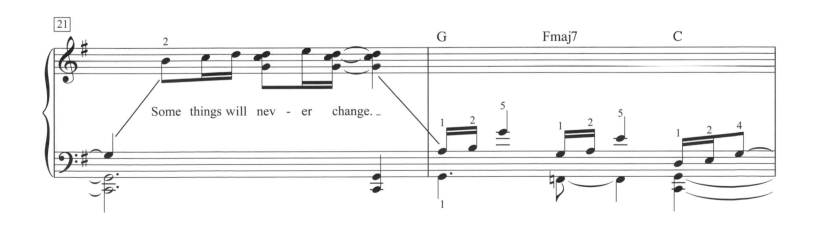

Some things will nev - er change. ___

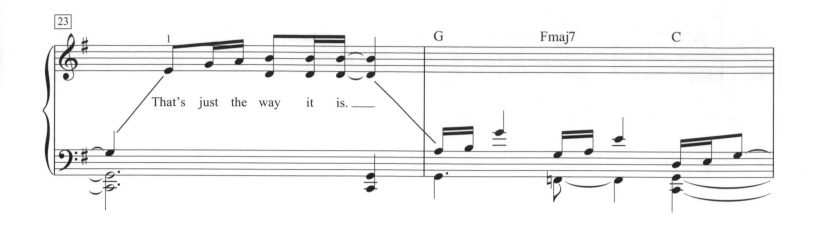

That's just the way it is. ___

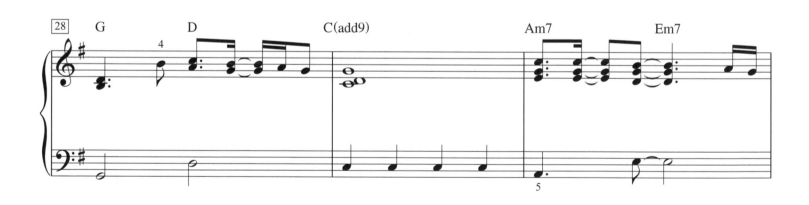

Ah, but don't you be - lieve ___ them. ___

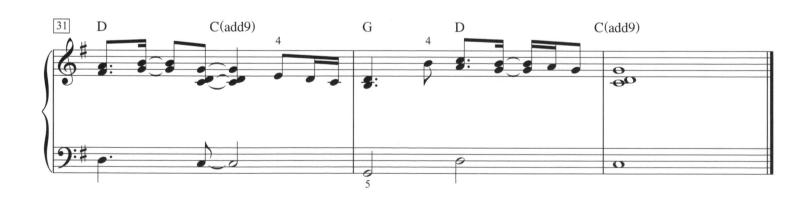